# Ruck Up with God!

## Dana P. McCloud, SGT (Ret.)

ISBN 978-1-68526-859-6 (Paperback)
ISBN 978-1-68526-862-6 (Digital)

Covenant Books
11661 Hwy 707
Murrells Inlet, SC 29576
www.covenantbooks.com

# ACKNOWLEDGMENTS

First and foremost, I desire to thank my Lord and Savior Jesus Christ for helping me put this book together.

To Brandy, you are the love of my life, best friend, confidante, and greatest supporter.

To my family and friends, thank you for believing in me and praying for me.

To Pastors Kenny Kuykendall and Shannon Irvin, thank you for your friendship and guidance.

To Crossroads and Gethsemane Baptist Churches, thank you for your prayers, love, and support.

To veterans of all services and wars, thank you for what you do and did. We fought the good fight, and now, it is time to forgive yourself and embrace peace!

Thank you.

# CONTENTS

Introduction ................................................................vii

Chapter 1:   Lima Charlie ..............................................1
Chapter 2:   PT ............................................................4
Chapter 3:   XO ...........................................................7
Chapter 4:   PX ............................................................9
Chapter 5:   The Plan ..................................................12
Chapter 6:   The 6 Ps ..................................................25
Chapter 7:   The Field Manual .....................................38
Chapter 8:   KISS Principle ..........................................41
Chapter 9:   Tactical Gear ............................................45
Chapter 10:  Packing List .............................................48
Chapter 11:  Battle Drills .............................................52
Chapter 12:  The Soldier, Et al. ....................................55
Chapter 13:  Valleys ....................................................67
Chapter 14:  Mountains ...............................................71
Chapter 15:  Battle Buddy ............................................74
Chapter 16:  Trust and Obey ........................................77
Chapter 17:  AAR .......................................................80

Afterword ................................................................83
References ................................................................85

Ken—

Thank you for your friendship and encouragement during the publication process.

It is my sincerest wish that you enjoy reading this book as much as I did writing it!

May the Lord continue to bless you, and I want you to know that you and your family are in Brandy and my prayers!

I look forward to strengthening our friendship and brotherhood in the Lord. Have a blessed and wonderful year!

Yours in Christ,

Dan

# INTRODUCTION

The content within this book serves to help with trauma from a soldier's perspective and the means to find peace and solace using God's Word. General William Tecumseh Sherman (1880) once said, "Some of you young men think that war is all glamour and glory, but let me tell you, boys, it is all hell!" His statement represents a constant but abhorrent truth. It often appears humanity prefers strife over peace—a need to take what others possess or place others in a position of submission for personal gain and conquest. I simply seek to help others find joy in this life once again, free from the memories that may or still haunt them.

Certain sections begin with acronyms while other concepts are familiar to those who wear or wore the uniform in the United States military; they represent a stressor/trigger and a suggested means of achieving victory over that stressor/trigger. If nothing else, the information provides some insight into how a person comes to accept a situation, gain peace with it over time, and realize others care about his or her well-being. The startling statistic of twenty-two suicides a day by service members serves as a stark reminder that our brothers and sisters in arms suffer in silence, often in our midst, and feel abandoned or afraid to say they need help. In response, I emphatically say, "I know and feel your pain, and I am here to help!" Forget the perceived stigma surrounding mental health; the only one who gets his or her mind right is you. Concerned friends and family assist and provide support, but the first step belongs to you.

I am reminded of Philippians 4:7 (KJV, 2011): "And the peace of God, which passeth all understanding, shall keep your hearts and minds through Christ Jesus." What happened and what you experienced cannot be taken from you; it becomes a part of you, but if you trust in God to help heal your mind, body, and soul, then peace and joy manifest themselves in your life. Forgive but not forget yourself!

# LIMA CHARLIE

The military alphabet produces a vast number of acronyms, some used in different contexts for a different branch of service. But in this case, Lima Charlie, sounds like lee-mah Charlee or LC, represents the shorter version of "loud and clear," and transcends all services as the response to the query of "radio check, over" on a military radio; older veterans probably remember saying, "Five by five." In other words, "Can you hear me clearly?" "Yes, I can."

The focus of chapter 1 involves what "Lima Charlie" represents, in this case, the concepts of loud and clear but not as it relates to communication. Loud, for the purpose of this chapter, involves the sound, noise, and, in some cases, lack of noise associated with combat or trauma. Whether you rode a tank across open country, fueled aircraft at an airbase, or manned the ambulance, the one constant for first responders involves *loud* noise. I know of other noise or lack of noise that prefaced either one or a barrage of loud noises. Improvised explosive devices, artillery, rockets, mortars, machine-gun fire, and even local traffic personify familiar and, in some cases, deafening sound.

Loud noise still makes us jump I bet, heads on a swivel, looking for the source, and standing down when we recognize the origin. But that reaction, a battle drill practiced over and over, becomes ingrained and acts closely with muscle memory. Let me simply say, "It is okay, and you're not alone." Some of you are reading this and saying to yourselves, "My reaction is super severe. I scare people." When facing such reactions, remind yourself of Psalm 27:1: "The Lord is my light and my salvation, whom shall I fear? The Lord is the strength of my life; of whom shall I be afraid?" Take this moment to reflect on him—the one who brought you home from that faraway battlefield and never left you. And in this moment of reflection, I believe you experience calm, the letter C for "Charlie."

Calm does not always mean deep serenity; occasionally, it turns out to be more of a pause, a time to collect one's thoughts and subdue anger, anxiety, and other venomous thoughts and actions. God hears you when you call to him; Psalm 107:28–29 says, "Then they cry out to the Lord in their trouble and he bringeth them out of their distresses. He maketh the storm a calm so that the waves thereof are still." God does this for us because he loves us and wants nothing to happen to his children.

I did mention serenity previously, a magnificent word defined by Webster's Dictionary (2017) as "the quality or state of being serene." In other words, free and clear of stormy weather or unpleasant change, utter calm. Pretty amazing to think. Let me illustrate it in another way. The scene in *Forrest Gump* where Lieutenant Dan Taylor, played by Gary Sinise, is tied into the crow's nest of the shrimp boat and challenging God to a showdown. Taylor's loss of his legs coupled with the ingrained legacy to fall on the field of battle with his men and the lack of shrimp catching productivity serve as the trigger for the showdown.

The storm that followed ravaged the shrimping industry along the bayou but left the boat of Forrest and Taylor afloat. Soon after, Taylor hopped off the boat and elementary backstroked into a beautiful sunset while Forrest narrated, "He never actually said it, but I think he made his peace with God." I am not advocating a full-blown test of wills with God, but he does hear you and only wants you to love him. I promise that God understands your fears, anger, and frustrations, and will help you, but you need to take the first step toward reconciliation.

Simply put, Romans 5:10 says, "For if, when we were enemies, we were reconciled to God by the death of His Son, much more, being reconciled we shall be saved by his life." The Apostle Paul clearly states that reconciliation with God occurs but only through his son Jesus Christ. To do this, one needs to ask for calm from above and simply call upon the name of Jesus.

Chapter 2

# PT

PT (pea tee) refers to physical training, the military version of a physical education class. PT involves exercises, team sports, calisthenics, and running, lots and lots of running. Recruits joining the military find themselves running from place to place quite often and occasionally *around* the post, base, or camp for a couple of hours at a time. Some service members like it, others not so much, but it does make for a more capable warrior.

However, our use of the acronym PT splits into punishment and time. We'll focus on punishment first; according to Webster's Dictionary (2017), punishment is (1) the act of punishing, (2a) suffering, pain, or loss that serves as retribution, (2b) a penalty inflicted on an offender through judicial procedure, and (3) severe, rough, or disastrous treatment. We'll focus on 2a and 3, specifically, and how a service member or first responder experiencing trauma puts themselves through suffering, pain, or loss that serves as retribution because of *self-administered* severe, rough, or disastrous treatment. Many times, we ask ourselves questions regarding the incidents of the trauma we experience by starting with Why? Why did I survive and not them?

Why did we get hit? Didn't we treat the locals with fairness and respect? Why am I here in this country? As a sufferer of survivor's guilt, I can plainly admit I asked *why* many times. This question leads to others like, What could I/we have done different so Joe could be here with me/us? Why couldn't I get someone in my chain of command to listen to my intelligence reports regarding a particular location?

All of these are self-inflicted forms of punishment, and because of our humanity, they are perfectly normal and expected to a point. But when does it become unhealthy and affect us in a manner where we lose our sense of self? A year? Two? Ten or more? I do not know that answer, but I do know many of our brothers and sisters in arms are suffering greatly because of this, punishing themselves for actions occurring in the chaotic and turbulent drama known as combat. Friends often describe nights of horrible dreams, visions of long since passed former comrades, and replays of scenarios so vivid; Hollywood could never come close to reenacting them in a millennium. No matter what you call them and how psychologists define them, I view them as a self-imposed punishment. In my situation, I asked God to forgive me, and I *know* he did, but why couldn't I forgive myself? Did I believe I am more entitled to suffer on earth even if God in heaven forgave me? I eventually forgave myself and found a scripture that reminded me of the length and breadth of God's forgiveness.

Ephesians 1:6–7 says, "To the praise of the glory of his grace, wherein he hath made us accepted in the beloved. In whom we have redemption through his blood, the forgiveness of sins according to the riches of his grace." Listen up, people, his grace is sufficient. His grace is sufficient and requires very little of our time—the *T* in our acronym pair.

Time is the one thing everyone claims not to have, but according to Pastor Kenny Kuykendall, from a sermon on a warm July Sunday morning in 2017, "God gives us 365 days with 24 hours in each day, and that equates to 525,600 minutes a year." I submit to you that time, as it relates to self-inflicted punishment, remains a valuable resource to help lessen the burden.

To throw off your chains or yoke, so to speak, you need to discover that every minute counts in our life and that you mean something to someone, somewhere. I touched on the national average of twenty-two suicides by veterans a day in the introduction—a horrifying but a sobering statistic.

I believe if God gives us 525,600 minutes in a year, then use some of them to get help. How many minutes does it take to type "help me" into a phone and send it to a friend or dial 1-800-273-8255, press 1 or text 838255 for the National Veteran's Crisis Line. The Veterans Administration also has prompts within its automated phone directory to redirect those contemplating suicide; it remains crucial that if someone needs help, they receive it with no shame or stigma attached.

And hope maketh not ashamed; because the love of God is shed abroad in our hearts by the Holy Ghost which is given unto us. (Romans 5:5 KJV, 2011)

Chapter 3

# XO

The acronym XO (ex oh) represents the second in command; the XO, in conjunction with the headquarters platoon staff, maintains accountability of personnel and equipment at his or her assigned level and makes mission-critical decisions regarding supply, administration, and maintenance.

However, I choose to refer to XO as *ex*haustion and *o*bservation. Let's look at exhaustion for a moment, especially in the context of dealing with trauma, and it points to "a state of extreme physical or mental fatigue" (Webster's, 2017). Over the years, it does not matter what era of a service member or first responder you represent; exhaustion plagues you and pushes you into short periods of depression and anxiety if you remain honest with yourself. Some of us choose activities, both healthy and unhealthy, to ward off the feelings associated with depression and anxiety, and those choices help and hinder us. We will go into greater detail about those activities in the next chapter, but for now, agree that some form of activity occurs and you do something to mask the depression and anxiety.

I chose the word mask because many of us, at one time or another, applied camouflage paint to our faces in an effort to conceal "shiny spots" and escape detection by an enemy force. What I want us to do, while camouflaged anyway, is take a moment and polish off our skills of *observation.* When looking at our actions while camouflaged, what do we observe exactly? Do we recognize the particular triggers that set our anxiety into motion, and if we see them, what action on contact do we use to defend ourselves from the assault? I wonder who or what we seek when the attack appears imminent, and we desire to solve the problem in the quickest manner possible knowing the attack most likely occurs again and again. Isaiah 41:13 (KJV, 2011) reminds us, "For I the Lord thy God will hold thy right hand, saying unto thee, Fear not; I will help thee." With these thoughts in mind, perhaps, now we require a trip to the PX.

Chapter 4

# PX

PX (Pea Ex), the acronym denotes the *post exchange*, names the military version of a department store where one can buy anything from toothpaste to the latest laptop computers. I am sorry to burst bubbles because a trip to the PX often does wonders for service members recently returning from field training exercises. The journey to the PX I want you to take involves identifying your *practices* and coming up with alternative e*x*ercises or retain particular activities to help deal with the anxieties you observe.

Practices, as a verb, means to "carry out or perform (a particular activity, method, or custom) habitually or regularly" (Webster's, 2017). In other words, we face a particular trigger to our anxiety, and we choose to practice drinking liquor or beer, often to excess, in an effort to deaden the pain and feelings welling up within us. Over time, adult beverages lose the power to ease the pain, and a person practices consuming prescription medication or illicit drugs.

Sometimes, a person practices mixing the two and ends up in recovery at best or taking his or her life, even accidentally, at worst. Many people practice other kinds of temporary pleasure activities, much to the concern of family and friends, like an excessive search for and consumption of pornography or frequenting prostitutes in an effort to replace feelings of guilt. Much like drugs and alcohol, the spirit of lust can result in an addiction that corrupts emotionally and spiritually. Overeating, gluttony if you will, represents the activity that plagues me the most. Not so much a comfort to my problems and issues but rather an inability to stop eating so heavily. At one point in my life, while still in uniform, mind you, I weighed in at a whopping 354 pounds during a Soldiers Readiness Program (SRP).

By all accounts, those in my chain of command possessed the ability to remove me from service but chose to counsel me and help me get closer to a healthier weight. I am thankful for the collective restraint shown by my leadership not to "kick me out," and I am also thankful to them for allowing me to retire with honor and dignity. Ironically, it took a photo of my wife and I from Christmas of 2015, fourteen months after I retired, to serve as a reality check and motivation to get serious about nutrition, exercise, and coming to grips with unhealthy behaviors.

During the writing of this book, I lost over one hundred pounds, performed some type of exercise daily, and reestablished my personal relationship with God.

I beseech you therefore, brethren, by the mercies of God, that ye present your bodies as a living sacrifice, holy, acceptable unto God, which is your reasonable service. And be not conformed to this world: but be ye transformed by the renewing of your mind that ye may prove what is that good, and acceptable, and perfect, will of God. (Romans 12:1–2 KJV, 2011)

Conversely, others choose to exercise or practice on his or her short game on the local golf course. It comes down to choosing to practice acts that build the mind, spirit, or body which serve as healthier alternatives to destructive activities that possibly lead to becoming one of the twenty-two daily veteran suicides. Two choices but only one allows us to deal with our triggers in a sober and clear manner and remain vertical and breathing fresh air for many years to come.

I read something one Sunday morning from Runner's World (2017) that reinforces the need to push toward good habits: "We are what we repeatedly do. Excellence, then, is not an act, but a habit" (Aristotle). If you want to be whole again, truly beat the demons that taunt and torture you, then choose to fight and win. We served with the greatest team on the planet. I only ask that you make the choice to serve the one true God in heaven who loves you and wants to heal you completely.

Chapter 5

# THE PLAN

No matter the size of the mission received, leaders and persons in positions of responsibility establish a plan. One definition of a plan, according to Webster's Dictionary (2017), involves "an orderly arrangement of parts of an overall design or objective." We know we use a plan to seek a specific goal or objective like "Operation Overlord" during World War II which initiated the liberation of Europe from Axis occupation and control. We also know that the possessed numerous working parts are acting in concert with one another under specified timelines with the primary goal of establishing a beachhead on the shores of Western France. The plan worked, maybe not exactly as written on paper, and illustrated a move of audacity punctuated by human courage and a show of determination to not quit in the face of adversity. While not necessarily as large of a plan as Overlord, you need to know what you want to do about achieving a goal like living peacefully for the rest of your days. How does one plan against a faceless but insidious enemy? I suggest using what you know, and to me, that means writing and implementing an Operation Order.

When you need help or assistance, think of Joshua 1:6, 9 (KJV, 2011):

> Be strong and of a good courage: people shalt thou divide for an inheritance the land, which I swear unto their fathers to give them… Have I not commanded thee? Be strong and of a good courage; be not afraid, neither be thou dismayed: for the Lord thy God is with thee whithersoever thou goest.

An Operation Order or OPORD consists of five paragraphs that identifies and addresses actions taken by personnel to accomplish an objective as directed by a commander. It outlines the plan for combat operations and serves as a detailed guide written in a manner that the lowest ranking individual understands and could take command if the need ever were to arise.

Those five paragraphs and additional information are listed as follows:

1. Situation
    a. Enemy forces
        i. Situation (enemy, weather and terrain)
        ii. Capabilities
        iii. Probable course of action
    b. Friendly forces
        i. Mission of next higher unit

        ii. Mission of adjacent units (left, right, front, rear)

        iii. Mission and location of supporting elements

    c. Attachments and Detachments

2. Mission, Who, What, When, Why, and Where (coordinates)

3. Execution

    a. Concept of operation

        i. Scheme of maneuver

        ii. Formation

        iii. Route

        iv. Tactical missions to subordinate units

    b. Subunit subparagraphs

    c. Coordinating instructions

4. Sustainment (formerly service support)

    a. Supply

        i. Rations

        ii. Uniforms and equipment

        iii. Arms and ammunition

        iv. Captured materiel

    b. Transportation

    c. Medical evacuation

    d. Personnel

    e. Prisoners of war

5. Command and Signal

    a. Signal.

        i. Frequencies and call signs.

        ii. Pyrotechnics and signals.

        iii. Challenge and password.

    iv.  Code words.
  b.  Command
    i.  Command leader location.
    ii.  Chain of command.

Now that I grabbed your attention and spurred memories of field training exercise preparation using sand tables and a plan written by your platoon leader, we need to modify the OPORD to something a little less complex like a FRAGO or fragmentary order. Most of us remembered and performed missions using these directives because the commander's intent remained unchanged, but the manner to achieve that objective ebbed and flowed like a river almost daily. When seeking a personal objective like peace, we need to know how to find and apply it to our daily lives. The FRAGO provides a guideline of just the five main paragraphs: situation, mission, execution, sustainment, and command and control.

Why don't we get started, and I advise writing it down. It does not require a major power point presentation but simply a 3 x 5 card or piece of notebook, paper, and a pencil. In an effort to achieve peace and mitigate the negative elements associated with trauma experience, we need to remember peace represents the objective sought and determine our situation. In this fight, each situation, while similar in nature, represents each of us singularly, personal to us, and includes an enemy seeking to dominate using familiar images, memories, sounds, and situations as weapons to wound and maim. For example, we desire to sleep peacefully, but our old friend depression attacks us when we close our eyes. We cannot fall asleep because depression hits the "play" button on our memories and savagely assaults us in an effort to gain dominance. Depression does not run solo either, oftentimes partnering with anxiety.

Depression seeks to remind of us our past while anxiety piles on with an uncertain future. Let me ask you to think about your past and then start with this question: What happened in your past that takes center stage on your present? Now consider your future, and I follow up with this question: What about tomorrow, a month from now, or ten years down the road that concerns you so much it disturbs your present? Perhaps knowing *exactly* what causes our emotions to spin forces us to react in a manner that dramatically affects daily functioning, allows us to name our "enemy," and gives us an opportunity to confront it. From the time we enter our service of choice, we learn about accountability and taking ownership of our situation. I encourage you to do that and remember Proverbs 3:21–24 (KJV, 2011):

> My son, let not them depart from thine eyes: keep sound wisdom and discretion: So shall they be life unto thy soul, and grace to thy neck. Then shalt thou walk in thy way safely and thy foot shall not stumble. When thou liest down, thou shalt not be afraid: yea, thou shalt lie down, and thy sleep shall be sweet.

When we identify the *situation* in which we find our-selves, deciding on an appropriate course of action makes logical sense. We develop a mission statement that seeks to answer the five Ws: who, what, when, where, and why. Knowing the answers or knowing how to get the answers requires some honesty with one's self; it is now gut check time with some related spiritual pain and possible tears. Hear me now: healing requires some form of grief, but no timeline exists as to when this occurs. Sometimes, an emotional breakdown happens many years after the trauma; the brain, in an effort for preservation of the person, puts up a temporary wall. Temporary, though, reflects just that, and what remains behind the wall comes to the forefront and demands our attention. Do not ignore it; embrace it, and determine the information that answers the five Ws.

I subscribe to leading by example, so it seems fair to offer my situation as the model for this exercise. Let me preface this by saying that in no way am I minimizing my fallen brethren's ultimate sacrifice in defense of freedom and a restoration of peace in Iraq. Rather, my situation involves me taking on a greater personal responsibility for the loss of three service members to a preventable accident because I felt like the information provided to higher command required immediate attention and faster action. I harbored a fair amount of resentment after the accident. Many of us feel that way I bet.

Some of us look back and question our ability to communicate effectively to the proper authority the importance of watching northbound traffic patterns into Kabul on Fridays ending with "3" after morning call to prayer.

Our experience, knowledge, and analysis of the intelligence tell us of an imminent vehicle-borne improvised explosive device (VBIED) attack for example. Seems farfetched and better suited for a fiction novel, but you understand my point. For me, the information I regularly reported involved twelve-digit grid coordinates of improvised explosive device (IED) holes as well as any other ground feature deemed unsafe to American and coalition ground forces. Initially, command directed that grid coordinates with a corresponding summary of severity of each spot sufficed, but then the scope widened to photographs and eventually expanded to measurements for proper perspective.

All of this made sense; deny the ability of the enemy to reuse the road to bury IEDs. I cannot give exact numbers, but I do know, at one point, we surveyed at least thirty-six holes and identified several danger areas including the one I am about to describe.

This particular danger spot started as a sinkhole and, over a period of a few weeks, eroded away by nearly ten feet leaving a gaping hole and exposing a water pipe. Dutifully, pictures, coordinates, and summaries served as the main points to many missions, often with suggested courses of action for repair, but no mission to provide security for the repair ever transpired. Soldiers talk of course, and rumors grind about diversion of the engineers to some main base project. I understood about priority of work and the use of resources and assets, but even the placement of concrete barriers as a quick fix worked in the interim. Meanwhile, recording and reporting of the danger areas continued, most often as a subordinate task to patrolling or checking on Iraqi military checkpoints. The repair never took place prior to August 15, 2005, and the aforementioned quick fix occurred about two days later, three days too late in my opinion.

I held on to this for over twelve years, taking responsibility for something I could not control, and blaming myself for not acting with more assertiveness. I felt like I let those guys down, that my information coupled with my reputation more than served as credibility to the severity of the threat. I also understood that commanders make decisions every day, determine where best to use personnel and equipment, but for me, that spot represented a known trouble area, and the rollover and loss of three soldiers on August 15, 2005, served to support my beliefs. The follow-on of the concrete barriers just added fuel to a cynical fire that burned deep in my gut. Accident or not, it bears repeating: those three soldiers gave their lives in defense of this great nation and for the safety and security for the people of Iraq, and I will never forget them. John 15:13 says, "Greater love hath no man than this, that a man lay down his life for his friends" (KJV, 2011). We know Jesus spoke about his impending death by crucifixion on Golgotha and the love he shared with the world through that sacrifice for us all. I also believe Jesus meant this for those, like the three brave men I mention, who gave up their lives freely so that the rest of us may live.

Now you see my situation—a misguided sense of responsibility and an extreme feeling of guilt. So what did I do about it, and how did I create a mission statement after all these years?

I took paper and pencil and drafted out the five Ws. It looked something like the following:

- Who—Dana P. McCloud
- What—forgiveness
- When—August 15, 2005
- Where—Iraq
- Why—gain peace

My mission is this: Dana P. McCloud asks for forgiveness for events related to the accident on August 15, 2005, in Mahmudiyah, Iraq, in order to regain physical, mental, and spiritual peace.

Simple but powerful. It's a single sentence that provides a starting point for the next phase in your healing: execution.

We now freely admit what we did, saw, or experienced and what we desire as an end state, but how do we get to it? If you remember the execution phase of the OPORD, that section discussed what routes we took, who was doing what, and what means of transportation took us there. This area requires very little thought but some planning, and a fair amount of patience and commitment. A journey starts with just one step. In other word, making a phone call to either the Veterans Administration or your personal physician. As far as the VA, I wholeheartedly encourage you to make the call and get yourself into the system. Once in the system, *tell* your provider *everything*; leave nothing out including mental health issues. You served your country, and you earned the care; don't be too proud to accept it or so humble you believe, like I did, that others require more help.

Despite a few bad instances of improper care at some VA hospitals and clinics, the VA really does care and truly wants to help all of us. We all remember hearing this at one time or another, "Be where you're supposed to be…at the appointed time." Give the Veterans Administration a chance to do it right.

When you are in need, especially when seeking medical help, 1 Peter 5:10 tells us, "But the God of all grace, who hath called us unto his eternal glory by Christ Jesus, after that ye have suffered a while, make you perfect, stablish, strengthen, settle you" (KJV, 2011).

If you do not choose the VA, at least see your general practitioner and request a mental health consult. I know; I know…the "stigma." In my opinion, this notion went the way of the dodo when the military introduced combat stress teams in the country. The army felt the need to incorporate them into the combat theater, and to my knowledge, no one I knew ever received retribution or discrimination for speaking to the doctor. Those who fear to tell a health-care provider that he or she suspects a mental health issue because an alleged stigma seems more afraid of coming to grips with the trauma and buy into this old school excuse. I know some occupations within the service require service members to be of sound mind especially in areas of national security, but those same jobs also require personnel to possess good general as well as sound mental health. Too often, in the past, the concept of mental health, as seen by the chain of command, equated to mental illness. Granted, both possess symptoms in common like withdrawal, but mental illness goes further in that the sufferer disconnects from reality. Generally, those who contend with PTSD remain fully aware of reality and often times exhibit hypervigilance or seek isolation in an effort to deal with it. I apologize for turning this toward a summary about mental health versus mental illness, but I strongly support anyone asking for help. If someone asks for it, the old excuse of stigma need not prevent them from getting it.

In this next section, sustainment, I thought about the elements an OPORD requires: supply, transportation, medical evacuation, personnel, and prisoners of war, but for the focus of this exercise, I think the support needed goes beyond the basic necessities of beans, bullets, and uniforms. We discussed the Veterans Administration and general practitioners previously—two resources I believe offer the best start for medical care for veterans, especially those suffering from trauma that needs addressing. Many of us suffer needlessly and become one of the twenty-two daily choosing suicide, unacceptable from where I sit. I know some organizations like the Veteran of Foreign Wars, American Legion, and Elks Club, for example, create small support groups that meet and talk about the trauma experienced—an outlet that works in conjunction with the medical care. The following organizations offer support groups for those looking to recover from trauma exposure and the corresponding debilitating symptoms. These organizations, and in no particular order, list as follows:

1. REBOOT Combat Recovery, P.O. Box 1223 Ft. Campbell, KY (931) 292–2011 info@rebootrecovery.com, http://www.rebootre-covery.com.
2. WRAP or The Wellness Recovery Action Plan found in most VA hospitals or clinics-https://www.mentalhealth.va.gov.
3. VA clinics—many offer recovery programs as part of daily operations.
4. Veterans Embracing Alternate Recovery Therapies, www.recovery.org specializing in alpha stimulation, equine recovery, Botox.

I know many of you question why I did not add a church, and I chose not to list it because, generally, church leadership does not understand the trauma current and former soldiers experience. My own pastor frankly admitted that he and many of his peers did not feel equipped to handle a member with such a serious affliction. I appreciated his candor and counseled him and his peers to listen for keywords and phrases but also offer relevant advice.

I am not telling any of you not to confide in your pastor or church leadership, talking to someone always helps, but what I am asking you to do involves exercising patience. All of them want to help you win this personal and internal war, and victory happens once they receive the appropriate set of tools and apply them in a manner that educates them about this insidious enemy.

The Lord is not slack concerning his promise, as some men count slackness, but is longsuffering toward us, not willing that any should perish, but that all should come to repentance. (2 Peter 3:9 KJV, 2011)

The last area in the OPORD, command, and signal, describes and establishes methods of communication, code words, passwords, and the chain of command for the operation. For this book, I chose to use acronyms service members and first responders recognize, and everyone else easily researches on the internet; it comes down to a simple means of communicating. Not many needs saying here, again simplicity with sending a message; however, everyone needs to use whatever form of communication necessary to ask for and receive the help they so desperately need.

As far as the chain of command, each person answers to him or herself but must remember others who care for you want to know how and what you plan to do both short and long-term. I also encourage you to say something; how much or little depends on personal choice. Do not feel compelled to say everything initially; however, even a little bit told today beats nothing said yesterday.

# Chapter 6

# THE 6 PS

No matter the service background from which you originate or your civilian field of endeavor, you most likely heard someone refer to "the six Ps." I recite them as "prior planning prevents purely poor performance," but several other colorful versions exist. My version of the six Ps provides a guideline to get closer to God, to ask him for anything, and to study his Word: the Bible.

My six Ps break down like this:

1. Prayer
2. Praise and
3. Patience
4. Perpetuate
5. Promises of
6. Peace

We'll look at the first P: prayer. Prayer, according to Webster's Dictionary (2017), is defined as "an address (such as a petition) to God, or an earnest request or wish." The easiest way to find God involves talking with him; God listens and wants to talk with us daily. God desires our attention, and the best means to commune with him involves prayer. Prayer involves practice, purpose, power, and persistence.

So how do we learn to pray? We practice. Anything we want to do well requires practice. Jesus taught us how to pray in Matthew 6:5–8, to pray in private and understand that God already knows our needs.

Jesus said,

> And when thou prayest, thou shalt not be as the hypocrites are: for they love to pray standing in the synagogues and in the corners of the streets, that they may be seen of men. Verily I say unto you, They have their reward. But thou, when thou prayest, enter into thy closet, and when thou hast shut thy door, pray to thy Father which is in secret; and thy Father which seeth in secret shall reward thee openly. But when ye pray, use not vain repetitions, as the heathen do: for they think that they shall be heard for their much speaking. Be not ye therefore like unto them: for your Father knoweth what things ye have need of, before ye ask him.

Say what is in your heart and mean it. Don't worry about fumbling with the words; God knows your intention, and he just wants to hear from you. Show him your love, compassion, sympathy, empathy, and intercession for others and. of course, your love for him. Praying pleases him, and with practice, your ability to pray becomes more natural and requires less effort.

When praying, *be specific* with your requests because like our own fathers, God wants to grant it. This is the purpose of prayer, and it serves as a means to communicate with God. We also need to remember to be sincere and virtuous in our prayers.

Paul told the congregation at Philippi, "Be careful for nothing, but in everything by prayer and supplication with thanksgiving, let your requests be made known to God. And the peace of God, which passeth all understanding, shall keep your hearts and minds through Jesus Christ" (Philippians 4:6–7 KJV, 2011).

One aspect that many forget involves thanking God for providing an answer to our prayer. Praising and thanking God for an answer, whether good or bad, confirms your sincerity with the prayer and your faith in God to answer it.

The Bible tells us in 2 Chronicles 20 that Jehoshaphat, king of Judah, faced a great multitude from afar, an invading army from the sea. He was fearful but came to the Lord and asked for help. Jehoshaphat, along with the tribe of Judah, prayed in verse 6, "And said, O Lord God of our fathers, art not thou God in heaven? and rulest not thou over all the kingdoms of the heathen? and in thine hand is there not power and might, so that none is able to withstand thee?" And God answered; the Holy Spirit within Jahaziel, a Levite of the sons of Asaph says in verse 15, "And he said, Hearken ye, all Judah, and ye inhabitants of Jerusalem, and thou King

Jehoshaphat, Thus saith the Lord unto you, Be not afraid or dismayed by reason of this great multitude; for the battle is not yours, but God's." Jehoshaphat and the people of Jerusalem knowing they need not fight, that the battle was won already, fell on their faces and worshipped God. The serious power of Judah's prayer was answered with divine power from God!

One must remember that God answers prayer in his time but sometimes does not grant every request or petition. This often causes a loss of faith or doubt that God does not hear him or her. I assure you that he always listens and wants us to talk to him but not strictly for what *we* want but also for what we desire for others. James 5:16 (KJV, 2011) supports this: "Confess your faults one to another, and pray one for another, that ye may be healed. The effectual fervent prayer of a righteous man availeth much." Show him you won't quit, that you'll pray continually, and "pray without ceasing" (1 Thessalonians 5:17 KJV, 2011). Do not think that unanswered prayer for you means God is not listening but rather consider the possibility he answered your prayer for the benefit of another. This is persistence!

Coming to God in humility and lifting up others pleases him so much.

> And this is the confidence that we have in
> Him, that if we ask any thing according to
> His will, he heareth us: And if we know that
> he heareth us, whatsoever we ask, we know

that we have the petitions that we desired of him. (1 John 5:14–15 KJV)

The second *P*, praise, represents an important and fulfilling aspect within our relationship with God. Praise, as a noun or a verb, is defined as "the offering of grateful homage in words or song, as an act of worship" (N.A., 2018). One can find a reference to praise 234 times in the Old Testament and 27 in the New Testament. The Hebrew word *Hallal*, the base word for Hallelujah as we know it, means "to be clear, to praise, to shine, to boast, show, to rave, celebrate, to be clamorously foolish" (Aglow International, 2018).

David wrote the following:

> While I live will I praise the LORD: I will sing praises unto my God while I have any being. (Psalm 146:2, KJV)

> Why art thou cast down, O my soul? and why art thou disquieted in me? hope thou in God: for I shall yet praise him for the help of his countenance. (Psalm 42:5 KJV)

Praise at its core includes four elements: acknowledgment, appreciation, adoration, and affection.

Acknowledge him for whatever circumstance you see yourself. Good or bad, give Him praise. Something went awry or sideways, and you're telling me to praise him? Absolutely! Give God the praise because we cannot make it in this world without his love, support, guidance, and affection. There are those out there who live life without God and appear to "have it all together," but I promise you, they don't. Behind closed doors, they suffer from anxiety, guilt, depression, loneliness, and feelings of abandonment. Once the doors open to the public, those same people act happy and give off the impression they have not a care in the world, but eventually, the façade cracks and crumbles. The psalmist wrote, "The Lord is my strength and my shield; my heart trusted in him, and I am helped: therefore my heart greatly rejoiceth; and with my song will I praise him" (Psalm 28:7 KJV).

Showing God your appreciation through praise ensures you actually feel happy as opposed to looking superficially happy. For me, I find comfort when praising God for everything I own and experience because, ultimately, he remains in control. Paul said, "Finally, brethren, whatsoever things are true, whatsoever things are honest, whatsoever things are just, whatsoever things are pure, whatsoever things are lovely, whatsoever things are of good report; if there be any virtue, and if there be any praise, think on these things" (Philippians 4:8 KJV).

With God, day-to-day living requires less effort and brings more joy. That in of itself demands praise and a deep show of adoration. Adoration, a noun, means the act of paying honor as to a divine being—worship, reverent homage and fervent and devoted love. Shout out to the Lord; thank him for all that he does for us. King David wrote, "Thou wilt shew me the path of life: in thy presence is fullness of joy; at thy right hand there are pleasures for evermore" (Psalm 16:11 KJV). David knew the Lord, experienced joy from his relationship with God and, as a result, praised him continually for the blessings bestowed on him and the kingdom of Israel. David adored God and praised him with music and song as a result. We know David wrote the book of Psalms, and it remains the best example of praise and worship in the Bible.

Affection means a fond attachment, devotion, or love for someone or something. It takes feeling, involves passion, whether good or bad, and lets us know we are alive. Paul wrote, "If ye then be risen with Christ, seek those things which are above, where Christ sitteth on the right hand of God. Set your affection on things above, not on things on the earth" (Colossians 3:1–2 KJV). Show God your love for him; don't just pay lip service.

> So being affectionately desirous of you, we were willing to have imparted unto you, not the gospel of God only, but also our own souls, because ye were dear unto us. (1 Thessalonians 2:8 KJV)

Who better to show unabashed, unashamed love, and affection than to our Father in heaven? Love him with reckless abandon!

Remember, acknowledgment, appreciation, adoration, and affection work together to make praise an integral part of our daily walk with God. Peter wrote,

> But ye are a chosen generation, a royal priesthood, an holy nation, a peculiar

people; that ye should shew forth the
praises of him who hath called you out of
darkness into his marvelous light: which
in time past were not as people, but are
now the people of God: which had not
obtained mercy, but now have obtained
mercy. (1 Peter 2:9–10 KJV)

I previously discussed prayer, one-on-one communication with God, in your prayer closet and making it a
daily habit. Secondly, we need to praise God, to worship
him, give him our honor, gratitude and love, use music,
instruments, clapping, whatever we choose to use. When
we put the first two into our walk with God, the third *P*,
patience, becomes part of the process. Patience is defined as
"perseverance; even-tempered care; diligence; the quality of
being patient." In my experience, especially when seeking
answers from God, patience requires a person to demonstrate discipline and faith. For many, patience represents
the least of God's gifts they wish to receive. Our society,
unfortunately, subscribes to "I want it, and I want it now,"
but trusting in the Lord to answer prayer or provide direction often takes time for which many of us cannot wait. I
am not suggesting that you just put your feet up and wait
for a sign, work, miracle, or wonder. God wants us to push
forward, to persevere in the face of adversity with his help,
and trust him to provide all of our needs within *his* time.
Hebrews 6:11–12 (KJV, 2017) tells us, "And we have desire
that every one of you do shew the same diligence to the
full assurance of hope unto the end: That ye be not sloth-

ful, but followers of them who through faith and patience inherit the promises."

Hebrews 6:11 uses the word *diligence,* and the definition of patience includes it. Diligence demonstrates an understanding of discipline and faith; we need these in abundance in order to exercise and implement patience. Discipline takes the most effort from us. It involves believing that God provides everything in his time, that you need not hasten anything from a position of desperation. *Not doing something because you trust God to provide often takes more willpower than quitting a harmful vice.* God wants us to need and rely on him, to genuinely take an interest in a relationship *with* him, but He also expects us to try to help ourselves and put forth an effort. First John 5:14–15 (KJV, 2017) supports this thinking: "And this is the confidence that we have in him, that if we ask any thing according to his will, he heareth us: And if we know that he hear us, whatsoever we ask, we know that we have the petitions that we desired of him." Circumstances and situations will change once you show some discipline as far as making time for and with God, to pray to him, praise him, and show some patience when asking for an answer.

If you demonstrate discipline in communing with God, then showing faith in him requires very little effort. Hebrews 11:1 says, "Now faith is the substance of things hoped for, the evidence of things not seen" (KJV, 2016). Faith that something or someone exists even when one cannot see those things takes discipline as well. But sometimes, our diligence in spending time with God, asking him for help or direction, does not result in outcomes we feel we deserve even to the point of questioning God's timing. In this, we question our faith and the strength of our relationship with the Father, but consider this: Hebrews 11:6 says, "But without faith it is impossible to please him: for he that cometh to God must believe that he is, and that he is a rewarder of them that diligently seek him."

On April 14, 2018, I, along with several others, ran a race at Lake Lanier Islands, the Fallen Heroes of Georgia 5K. I think I can safely speak for everyone when I say it was an extremely emotional experience. When I finished the race, I thought about Hebrews 12:1–2 (KJV, 2011):

> Wherefore seeing we also are compassed about with so great a cloud of witnesses, let us lay aside every weight, and the sin which doth so easily beset us, and let us run with patience the race that is set before us, Looking unto Jesus the author and finisher of our faith; who for the joy that was set before him endured the cross, despising the shame, and is set down at the right hand of the throne of God.

In other words, the race set before the Hebrews, according to Paul, requires them to persevere in the obedience of faith in Christ; depending on whether they accept, there is a crown of glory or everlasting misery as a reward, and we face the same challenge.

And it is by no means easy because, like on many racecourses, sin represents potholes and cracks in the pavement, obstacles meant to make us stumble, much like the sin we know we are most prone because of habit, age, or circumstances. This is a serious and important exhortation; whatever sin favors a man, whatever it might be, if it remains free to roam within him and not subdued, it prevents him from running the Christian race. It saps every reason for running and amplifies power to every discouragement. But there is good news because when we achieve a perfect state, we receive full reconciliation to God's rebuke of us. Because he loves us, God's correction does not equate to condemnation but rather, the chastening teaches patience and promotes great holiness. Simple and complex living all rolled into one.

"To preserve from extinction or oblivion" defines perpetuate, the fourth *P*. Perpetuate is a verb, and verbs represent action, and action involves movement and, as such, raises several questions. In our quest for internal peace, is it any wonder that an element of that search involves preventing something from ending? Do we seriously want to quit or allow our efforts to end either proverbially or in real death? Is that not what extinction means? Once we establish a joyful and loving relationship with God, do we not want that to perpetuate? Of course, we do because the benefits gained from prayer and praise vastly outweigh a life devoid of any blessings. Pray without ceasing; I also encourage you to praise without ceasing. To me, perpetuating prayer and praise results in a bounty of heavenly riches. An excellent example of this comes from Ezekiel 34:26 (KJV): "And I will make them and the places round about my hill a blessing; and I will cause the shower to comedown in his season;

there shall be showers of blessings." The promise of "showers of blessings" invokes images of abundant gifts provided by God, both earthly and heavenly. Pray to God; praise God for what you own and even for what you don't, and do so because it pleases him.

Promise, the fifth *P*, emphasizes the special nature of our relationship with God. Once we establish our connection and commune with him, we receive a *promise* from him in return. The Bible is full of God's promises; his written Word is a chronological reference from beginning to end. His promises are not finite; they serve to remind us of his love for us, that he will never leave nor forsake us. Even when *we* feel as though no hope exists, he offers an answer through scripture: "But the God of all grace, who hath called us unto his eternal glory by Christ Jesus, after that ye have suffered a while, make you perfect, stablish, strengthen, settle you" (1 Peter 5:10 KJV).

For every concern, he provides a promise in the form of scripture. Some key promises involve God's love, forgiveness, joy, strength, and the return of his Son, Jesus Christ, to name a few. God also provides answers to other situations and circumstances in our lives, good and bad. God wants us to rely on him, to come to him when we need help or comfort. We need to seek him and find solace in the knowledge that for every situation or opportunity we face, he offers wise counsel and advice perfect for our need. As we continue to seek internal peace for ourselves, we need to thank him for all of his promises, especially for his love. The apostle John wrote, "In this was manifested the love of God toward us, because that God sent his only begotten Son into the world, that we might live through him" (1 John 4:9 KJV).

Peace, the sixth *P*, represents the ultimate objective: a serenity given because we ask God to provide it for us. The peace we seek happens because we remain faithful in our relationship with God. When we pray regularly, take time to praise God for everything in our lives, and use patience when waiting on God's answer, we find that God, through the sending of the Holy Spirit, he grants us the peace we seek. We know that if God has it, we want it and abundantly. King David wrote in Psalm 29:11, "The Lord will give strength unto his people; the Lord will bless his people with peace" (KJV, 2011). God wants us to live in peace, to love one another as much as he loves us. For something so wonderful given freely, why do we seem to struggle so hard to receive it? The answer lies in Philippians 4:7 (KJV, 2011): "And the peace of God, which passeth all understanding, shall keep your hearts and mind through Christ Jesus." We have trouble receiving God's peace because we spend too much time focusing on the things of this world. When we put our eyes, heart, love, and time on Jesus, the rewards from heaven, specifically peace, are unfathomable. This plan takes serious practice, an open mind, and a forgiving heart, but nothing worth earning ever happens easy.

# Chapter 7

# THE FIELD MANUAL

Learning is an important part of life—a necessary function that allows us to grow intellectually. From the time we first enter school, reading, writing, and arithmetic account for a majority of our learning; as we get older, teachers introduce textbooks that assist us with learning new and occasionally complex concepts. The military offers much the same in the form of field manuals, even in the age of computers. A new recruit receives instruction from drill sergeants who in turn teach from the Soldier's Basic Common Tasks Manual. This book serves as a building block and a reference where a recruit finds the answer he or she seeks. The Bible serves Christians in the same manner and for the same reason: to find answers to questions. A soldier's "smart book," however, provides only finite answers to common relevant military questions whereas the Bible provides infinite answers to any number of questions. Is it any wonder that the Bible remains the best-selling book year after year?

The Bible is not just a book found in the drawer of a hotel nightstand or an account of the greatest story ever told. The Bible represents a written history of the ultimate authority on everything we see, hear, believe, and experience in our lives. The Bible breathes, gives us life in the form of wisdom, advice, and hope. Much like a military field manual, it provides useful information to help us learn about a subject, grow with the knowledge, and avoid mistakes when confronted with a particular situation. The Bible contains an unimaginable amount of information and serves as the most complete reference book ever written. It does not require an advanced degree or a fancy school in theology to understand but just a desire to read, pray, meditate, and study. The Bible stands alone on its merit; it should consider God chose regular men and women to write down what he told them. It exudes power, stands against the test of time and the critique of skeptics, councils, commissions, ideologies, and governments.

The easiest example to support this involves Jesus Christ before Pontius Pilate. All four gospels, Matthew 27, Mark 15, Luke 23, and John 18 confirm that Pontius Pilate found no fault in Jesus Christ, an innocent man, and left the decision to a rabid mob of people handpicked by Jesus's enemies. Pilate washed his hands of the decision and did not involve the Roman government in condemning Jesus to die. Pilate's own wife counseled against it in Matthew 27:19 (KJV, 2011), "When he was set down on the judgment seat, his wife sent unto him, saying, Have thou nothing to do with that just man: for I have suffered many things this day in a dream because of him." Pilate knew of and believed in Jesus's innocence in the entire matter; his wife, affected by the Holy Spirit, added credence to this fact, and Pilate made the political decision to leave condemnation to the Jews. Pilate publicly washes his hands in Matthew 27:24 confirming no government, specifically Rome, would ever stand against almighty God.

The Bible provides information that fosters comfort, love, peace, and everlasting salvation. Whatever your desire to learn or your search for an answer to an affliction, the Word of God provides answers just like a soldier's field manual.

# Chapter 8

# KISS PRINCIPLE

*K*eep *it s*imple, *S*imon (Peter).

This section came to me after a Sunday school lesson brought forth by a godly and kind man; I'll call him Larry. Larry spoke about entering heaven through Jesus and that he's the door we must pass through to attain our eternity with him. John 14:6 says, "Jesus saith unto him, I am the way, the truth, and the life: no man cometh unto the Father, but by me." From this passage, Jesus Christ encourages us to seek him out, to tell everyone that nothing supersedes the acceptance that Jesus's death means: our eternal life; good works, good intentions, and living right, while honorable, remain subordinate to the truth.

You're not getting to heaven simply because you did good things on earth; it doesn't work that way. It works in this manner; one acknowledges the "door," opens it, and passes through freely without concern or reservation. In other words, *believe* that Jesus *is* real, admit you are a sinner, and agree that he died for our sins; acknowledge that his blood at Calvary washed away *all* the sin within the world, and then establish a relationship with him. I place no stock in religion; however, I want to encourage you to begin a relationship with Jesus. Love him as he loves you. Be open, honest, and real with him; that's all he really desires from us. And once He knocks on the door, I encourage you to use the KISS principle: "Keep It Simple, Simon" (Peter) by opening it, walking through, and embracing Jesus! Imagine being Peter for an instant, always so near to Jesus, with the ability to speak with him and embrace him and believe him. He gave up his fishing nets and followed Jesus while not questioning or overthinking. So how do you keep it simple?

The Bible tells us in Matthew 16:24–28, "Then said Jesus unto his disciples, 'If any *man* will come after me, let him deny himself, and take up his cross, and follow me.'" (verse 24). A disciple of Christ follows him in duty and ultimately to glory; He or she walks in the same manner as Christ. The Holy Spirit acts as a guide, but the follower treads in His steps, and whither so he goes. "Let him deny himself." If self-denial represents a hard lesson, it's not even close to what the Master learned and practiced to redeem us and to show us: "Let him take up his cross."

> 25: "For whosoever can save his life shall lose it: and whosoever can lose his life for my sake shall realize it."
> 26: "For what's a person profited, if he shall gain the total world, and lose his own soul? or what shall a person give up exchange for his soul?"

Thousands lose their souls for the most trifling gain or the most worthless indulgence, usually from mere sloth and negligence. No matter that men desolate themselves from Christ, that's the value Satan buys their souls.

> 27: "For the Son of man shall come in the glory of his Father with his angels; sand then he shall reward every man according to his works."

Nonetheless one soul is value over all the planet. this is often Christ's judgment upon the matter; he knew the value of souls, for he saved them; nor would he misjudge the planet, for he created it.

> 28: "Verily I say unto you, There be some standing here, which shall not taste of death, till they see the Son of Man coming in his kingdom."

The dying offender cannot purchase one hour's respite to hunt mercy for his perishing soul. Allow us to then learn justly the worth of our souls and Christ because he is solely the Savior of them.

Jesus loves us; he wants us to follow his teachings to the best of our ability, and he offers eternal life freely without asking for anything in return. Make the choice and answer the door when he knocks. Revelations 3:20 tells us, "Behold, I stand at the door, and knock: if any man hear my voice, and open the door, I will come in to him, and will sup with him, and he with me" (N.A., 2019).

I promise that living for Christ makes all the difference in your life. Keep it simple, Simon; choose eternal life with Jesus because we possess no power to save ourselves, and none of us truly deserves to live forever in a burning lake of fire.

Chapter 9

# TACTICAL GEAR

TA-50 or table of allowances 50 refers to the authorized gear and equipment individuals receive from their unit, often occurring at a central issue facility or CIF. TA-50 encompasses the uniforms one wears, the tactical equipment relevant to mission or deployment, and nearly full body armor designed to protect against direct fire, indirect fire, and improvised explosive devices. Without a uniform, a soldier stands apart from his or her colleagues, and without the appropriate equipment, a soldier fails to successfully accomplish a mission or runs the risk of receiving an injury.

Those seeking peace and wanting to achieve victory over the specters of the past must possess relevant equipment and a "uniform" as it were. The Bible tells us in Ephesians 6:10, 11 (KJV), "Finally my brethren, be strong in the Lord, and in the power of His might. Put on the whole armor of God, that ye may be able to stand against the wiles of the devil." This is a formal call for us to receive both tangible and spiritual gifts needed to protect ourselves from the attacks of the enemy. Furthermore, scripture states, "For we wrestle not against flesh and blood, but against principalities, against powers, against the rulers of the darkness of the world, against spiritual wickedness in high places" (Ephesians 6:12 KJV).

Our thoughts and feelings about a particular time in our lives work in concert with one another to serve as a memory, whether pleasant or not. We must also remember that the enemy uses these memories to serve a purpose, to drive a wedge within us, seek our end by planting obstacles like doubt and guilt. This attack seems relentless to the point where the enemy pushes us toward a decision, one self-serving and final.

> Wherefore take unto you the whole armour of God, that ye may be able to withstand in the evil day, and having done all, to stand. (Ephesians 6:13 KJV)

Make no mistake, the world remains at a constant state of spiritual war, and the people on this earth fall victim to attacks of differing kinds and sizes daily. There are those of you who believe me, and I also realize that to some of you, what I suggest sounds peculiar, far-fetched, or doubtful. I expect those reactions, but I assure you, those of us living here now experience spiritual attacks from an unseen enemy. This enemy goes by many names: Satan, Beelzebub, Lucifer, the Serpent, Roaring Lion, and the Beast. The enemy possesses an army, one that seeks to destroy the world of man by any means necessary.

This army of evil spirits and demons identifies and manipulates our weaknesses. This army moves against us in many ways using a myriad of tactics with the goal of defeating us. This army uses our own habits, vices, fears, anxieties, memories, inhibitions, and feelings against us—a relentless attack on our minds, bodies, and souls. So how do we repel these attacks? What equipment can be issued to fight this war and gain victory over the enemy? I submit to you that gaining victory begins with a very familiar Bible verse: "For God so loved the world, that he gave his only Son, that whosoever believeth in him should not perish, but have everlasting life" (John 3:16 KJV, 2011). The counterattack, if you will, begins with believing in Jesus Christ and calling on him to help battle the demon army of the enemy.

You and I cannot fight alone, we do not possess the spiritual strength to fight a battle against Satan one-on-one. Lest we forget, Satan has studied and twisted humanity since the days of Adam and Eve in the garden of Eden. His attacks take many forms, most often subtle but also overt, and occur repeatedly or at random. This enemy possesses no readily expected pattern of attack, and yet it is discernible which means, with training, an individual properly equipped can protect him or herself.

# Chapter 10

# PACKING LIST

A packing list represents an itemized grocery list, if you will, of the basic items required for a soldier to successfully complete a field training exercise or FTX; these events occur periodically during a soldier's time of service. Of course, seasoned soldiers know to bring other essential personal items like baby wipes, for example, because we all know "cleanliness is next to Godliness. Other soldiers bring extra food; pogey bait is the commonly known term or military specification (MilSpec), authorized clothing, and equipment because it's better to have and not need it than to need it and not have it. Experience, experience, experience, becomes the name of the game when packing one's gear to accomplish a mission with relative comfort and protection from the elements.

I suggest using some common sense when packing especially when confronted with cold, rainy, or hot weather. It just pays to know exactly what type of outer garment handles whatever weather one faces and making the best all-around choice so one does not feel miserable.

But what do you need to pack when facing the daily spiritual elements of this world? I say start simple, maybe three main ideas like fundamentals, follow through, and fellowship.

I'm sure opinions vary, but I advise using the fundamentals: perform a daily devotion or a chapter study within one of the Bible's books then pray. To prepare for the day, read, read, read! God's Word provides answers to the things we face, seen and unseen.

Here are a few examples: Feeling guilty? Read Hebrews 10:22–23 or Ephesians 3:12. Dealing with anxiety? Psalm 55:22, Philippians 4:6–7, or 1 Peter 5:7. You desire revenge? Proverbs 25:21–22. You struggle with addiction? Proverbs 23:29–35 and Romans 6:1–23, or perhaps things are going well? Job 31:24–28; Proverbs 15:27; 1 Timothy 6:18–19, and Hebrews 13:5. Yes, even good things require your attention and deserve just as much effort from you to handle. Just because of human nature, we often choose to silently deal with the good stuff while vocally expressing our disdain or misery for the bad stuff we face. Praise just as loud for the good things, and maybe complain.

The second we include on our packing list is follow through. Keep it up, keep trying, and when adversity pushes you, shove back *hard!* The key to this, like any endeavor that requires consistency, involves not giving up, or if you miss a day, start again the next. Second Thessalonians 2:16–17 says, "Now our Lord Jesus Christ himself, and God, even our Father, which hath loved us, and hath given *us* everlasting consolation and good hope through grace, comfort your hearts, and stablish you in every good word and work (KJV, 2017).

The third aspect of fellowship involves meeting other like-minded people who share the similar beliefs. Over the years, I've repeatedly heard the phrase, "I fellowship directly with God. I don't need church or others to prove my belief." I strongly disagree with this position when one deals with the issues of daily life for several reasons. In general terms, humans are social creatures and enjoy the company of others, sharing with each other the happenings of their lives both good and bad. Those you meet within church share similar beliefs, morals, and social norms; they become an extension of your family and often know more about you than your actual family.

Secondly, God's Word in 2 Corinthians 8:4 says, "Praying us with much intreaty that we would receive the gift, and take upon us the fellowship of the ministering to the saints" (KJV, 2017). We need to gather together, to worship and praise, to hear his word spoken from an anointed man of God and remember what we mean to one another.

Thirdly, church not only encompasses a physical building but also the gathering of people inside—the people inside truly representing the definition of church. Second Corinthians 6:14 reinforces this train of thought, "Be ye not unequally yoked together with unbelievers: for what fellowship hath righteousness with unrighteousness? and what communion hath light with darkness?" (KJV, 2017). It's good for the soul to meet with others; it's a way to strengthen one's consistency to meet other believers. We need each other; we need to meet and commune with one another, and do our level best to minimize isolating ourselves. I would never condemn a person for his or her way to celebrate the Lord, but intentionally choosing to celebrate with the purpose of avoiding others seems selfish to me. I just feel that the person choosing to be alone is missing out on what others might offer, and those others miss out on what that person offers to the group as well.

The Apostle John says it best in several verses in 1 John chapter 1: "Which we have seen and heard declare we unto you, that ye also may have fellowship with us: and truly our fellowship is with the Father, and with his Son Jesus Christ," and verses 6 and 7, "If we say that we have fellowship with him, and walk in darkness, we lie, and do not the truth: But if we walk in the light, as he is in the light, we have fellowship one with another, and the blood of Jesus Christ his Son cleanseth us from all sin" (KJV, 2017).

Fellowship is an act of obedience; seeing others pleases him, reinforces our relationship with him, and does not serve as a weekly *checkbox*. Do it because you want to do it, not because you feel guilt or coercion or feel obligated. I do it because I love those I call my church family, and I can talk with them as often as I want, not just on Sundays and Wednesday evenings.

Chapter 11

# BATTLE DRILLS

When we prepare to go overseas during pre-deployment training, we learn, practice, and perform battle drills so when a situation arises, we know how to respond appropriately. Not all of us cleared our first room correctly; sometimes, it took ten or more tries, but eventually, the practice turns to muscle memory, and that results in the successful completion of the task. Ultimately, we learn these drills to engage an enemy and save lives. The same can be said when we prepare to go out into the world in our daily lives.

When living for God, seeking his comfort, and praying for peace, we also need to learn, practice, and perform battle drills. Much like any required task, we need to remember to suit up, ensure the serviceability of our equipment, know the plan, and take the objective.

The key here involves the repetition of daily tasks like devotional and prayer for example and knowing how to press forward to face the day. Every one of us exhibits differences in how we approach a daily regimen, but we do something. Consider your morning routine, break down what you do in minutes, and determine the total time to accomplish those tasks.

Once you figure out the time taken, look at the list again, and apply the actual time you need to make breakfast, wash your face, and watch the news. Here's an easy one for most of us. Cut out browsing social media in the morning and wait until your first break at work. I believe that activity alone gives you fifteen to thirty minutes; it's more than enough time to pray, read a daily devotional, or study scripture—fifteen to thirty minutes preparation to face the day with the full power of God at your side. Can you imagine the tasks, jobs, and chores you complete *every* day when you begin the day with your Father in heaven?

Matthew 28:20 (KJV, 2011) says this, "Teaching them to observe all things whatsoever I have commanded you: and lo, I am with you always, even unto the end of the world. Amen." Jesus said this; Matthew emphatically states that Jesus did, and we also know that he started his day talking with his father. Not to make light of it, but Jesus performed a daily battle drill as confirmed by Mark 1:35 (KJV, 2011), "And in the morning, rising up a great while before day, he went out, and departed into a solitary place, and there prayed." Jesus spent time with God as part of his day, an important part despite his busy schedule, and made it a habit. In our pursuit of internal peace, would it not seem like a good idea to prepare as Jesus did daily?

This sacrifice of Jesus's time pleased God, and by following his perfect example, we please God as well. What do you honestly lose by spending time with God? Nothing whatsoever I assure you because the gain of salvation out-weighs anything this world provides. There is no peace in the world without first acknowledging the sacrifice of the Prince of Peace, the Lord, and Savior Jesus Christ.

Chapter 12

# THE SOLDIER, ET AL.

Before I get into this chapter, I want everyone to know that I value each one of you regardless of branch of service. No matter whether you enlisted or received a commission, you served with honor, distinction, and performed your duty admirably. I thank you for making the choice to serve and ask each of you to fondly remember your service to this great nation. No one can take that away from you, and donning the uniform ties all of us together in an unbreakable bond earned from the shedding of blood, sweat, and tears.

For most of us, our time as a soldier, sailor, airman, or marine represents a period of our lives where we often believe in something greater than ourselves. That's the key: a belief in something greater than ourselves and, for most of us, having faith in your teammates and platoon members to do their jobs and watch out for one another. But I am now asking you to believe in someone infinitely greater than each of us, and this person goes by the name of Jesus Christ, the Son of God.

As service members, we believe we can win anything anytime and because we commit everything that represents us to achieving our goals and accomplishing the mission. And yes, we often do so in blind faith: receiving information on good authority from people we trust and acting on it because we believe in what we do wholeheartedly. No difference exists when you freely choose to believe in and walk with Jesus Christ; you take a chance and discover a whole new life with the One who died for you on Golgotha's Hill at a place called Calvary.

I assure you that his death ensures our everlasting life, and all you need to commit to involves in believing that Jesus did die on the cross for your, mine, *our* sins, and after three days resurrected from the dead. As service members, we believed in much less significant ideas with as much passion and fervor as a rabid sports fan. I know what you think, and I hear questions all the time like these: "So how does blind faith in Jesus relate to my service?" "I'm broken emotionally, physically, mentally, and spiritually, why would Jesus want me in any capacity?" The most common is, "Why would Jesus forgive me for the things I've done when I can't forgive myself?" Take it from me; Jesus loves service members almost as much as he does little children. Jesus loving kids requires little effort to understand; kids generally express great innocence and wonder and not influenced by the ways of the world. But soldiers, sailors, airmen, and marines, Jesus really loves us? Yes, the God of the Valley remains the same as the God of the Mountain, and he appreciates our discipline, enthusiasm, and commitment to our beliefs and values.

From the moment of taking our oath of service, our lives change dramatically and generally require us to lose our individuality and embrace the concept of working with others to pass basic training and our specific job schools. Depending on others to get through training, even in small amounts, relates directly to relying on God to get us through life. He finds the strength of our conviction to an ideal, and the reliance on others encouraging, precursors to finding a higher purpose as time and our lives go forward. As I get older, I find more of my friends and former comrades in arms making the wonderful decision to leave themselves behind, believe in Jesus Christ, and take up his cross to serve him.

I encourage you to choose Christ, to walk with him daily because I know how he changed me, made me "a new creature" and that he forgave me for *everything* when he died on the cross. This does not mean I'm perfect, but he is, and his grace is sufficient.

As service members, we recognize leadership and follow orders those leaders give because we believe in those in charge. Choosing to believe in Jesus, exhibiting faith in his leadership and abilities to provide for us requires less effort than when we served, but doing so guarantees a much greater reward.

I assure you that God really loves soldiers and warriors. Exodus 17:10 (KJV, 2017) puts the battle of Joshua against the Amalek into context:

And he called the name of the place Massah, and Meribah, because of the chiding of the children of Israel, and because they tempted the LORD, saying,

Is the LORD among us, or not? Then came Amalek, and fought with Israel in Rephidim. And Moses said unto Joshua, Choose us out men, and go out, fight with Amalek: tomorrow I will stand on the top of the hill with the rod of God in mine hand. So Joshua did as Moses had said to him, and fought with Amalek: and Moses, Aaron, and Hur went up to the top of the hill. And it came to pass, when Moses held up his hand, that Israel prevailed: and when he let down his hand, Amalek prevailed. But Moses' hands were heavy; and they took a stone, and put it under him, and he sat thereon; and Aaron and Hur stayed up his hands, the one on the one side, and the other on the other side; and his hands were steady until the going down of the sun. And Joshua discomfited Amalek and his people with the edge of the sword.

Jehoshaphat, in 2 Chronicles chapter 20 is about "the victory over the Ammonites, Moabites, and inhabitants of Mount Seir."

Consider God's promise to Joshua of a victory over Jericho: Joshua 6 tells us what God wanted Joshua and the people of Israel to do to ensure that victory, specifically from verse 15:

And it came to pass on the seventh day, that they rose early about the dawning of the day, and compassed the city after the same manner seven times: only on that day they compassed the city seven times.

And it came to pass at the seventh time, when the priests blew with the trumpets, Joshua said unto the people, Shout; for the Lord hath given you the city.

And the city shall be accursed, even it, and all that are therein, to the Lord: only Rahab the harlot shall live, she and all that are with her in the house, because she hid the messengers that we sent.

And ye, in any wise keep yourselves from the accursed thing, lest ye make yourselves accursed, when ye take of the accursed thing, and make the camp of Israel a curse, and trouble it.

But all the silver, and gold, and vessels of brass and iron, are consecrated unto the Lord: they shall come into the treasury of the Lord.

So the people shouted when the priests blew with the trumpets: and it came to pass, when the people heard the sound of the trumpet, and the people shouted with a great shout, that the wall fell down flat, so that the people went up into the city, every man straight before him, and they took the city.

And they utterly destroyed all that was in the city, both man and woman, young and old, and ox, and sheep, and ass, with the edge of the sword. (Joshua 6:15–21)

And why did the walls fall? Because like a good soldier, Joshua trusted and obeyed his commander and followed his commands without question.

Here's another example that many of us know: young David slaying the giant Philistine, Goliath; 1 Samuel chapter 17 tells the story of young David slaying a Gath named Goliath, "And the Philistine said, I defy the armies of Israel this day; give me a man, that we may fight together" (KJV, 2017).

David was the fourth son of Jesse, but David stayed behind to look after the sheep in Bethlehem while his three older brothers fought for King Saul. For forty days, Goliath goaded Saul's army, mocking God, and calling out for anyone to fight him in the open field. David brought provisions for his brothers at the battle as Jesse commanded, and David heard the disrespectful taunts of the Philistine. David asked a crowd of men what Saul might do to the one who took on and defeated the giant, and those within the crowd said Saul would offer great riches. And again, Goliath goaded the men and army of Israel, "And David said, What have I now done? Is there not a cause?" (verse

29). Because of his righteous anger and a heart after God's own, David stood up and told Saul he would cut down this Philistine as easily as God helped him defeat a bear and a lion in the wilderness while protecting his flock of sheep. In response, Saul provided David with a full kit of armor and weapons, but all were too big, or as in David's words, "I cannot go with these; for I have not proved them. And David put them off him" (verse 39). This leads us to the actual battle starting in verse 40:

> And he took his staff in his hand, and chose him five smooth stones out of the brook, and put them in a shepherd's bag which he had, even in a scrip; and his sling was in his hand: and he drew near to the Philistine.
>
> And the Philistine came on and drew near unto David; and the man that bare the shield went before him.
>
> And when the Philistine looked about, and saw David, he disdained him: for he was but a youth, and ruddy, and of a fair countenance.
>
> And the Philistine said unto David, Am I a dog, that thou comest to me with staves? And the Philistine cursed David by his gods.
>
> And the Philistine said to David, Come to me, and I will give thy flesh unto

the fowls of the air, and to the beasts of the field.

Then said David to the Philistine, Thou comest to me with a sword, and with a spear, and with a shield: but I come to thee in the name of the Lord of hosts, the God of the armies of Israel, whom thou hast defied.

This day will the Lord deliver thee into mine hand; and I will smite thee, and take thine head from thee; and I will give the carcases of the host of the Philistines this day unto the fowls of the air, and to the wild beasts of the earth; that all the earth may know that there is a God in Israel.

And all this assembly shall know that the Lord saveth not with sword and spear: for the battle is the Lord's, and he will give you into our hands.

And it came to pass, when the Philistine arose, and came and drew nigh to meet David, that David hasted, and ran toward the army to meet the Philistine.

And David put his hand in his bag, and took thence a stone, and slang it, and smote the Philistine in his forehead, that the stone sunk into his forehead; and he fell upon his face to the earth.

So David prevailed over the Philistine with a sling and with a stone, and smote the Philistine, and slew him; but there was no sword in the hand of David.

Therefore David ran, and stood upon the Philistine, and took his sword, and drew it out of the sheath thereof, and slew him, and cut off his head therewith. And when the Philistines saw their champion was dead, they fled. (1 Samuel 17:40–51)

See how frail and uncertain life is, even when a man (Goliath) thinks himself best fortified; how quickly, how easily, and by how small a matter, the passage may be opened for life to go out and death to enter. Let not the strong man glory in his strength nor the armed man in his armor. God resists the proud and pours contempt on those who defy him and his people. No one ever hardened his heart against God and prospered. David *believed* God would deliver Goliath to him, and he did in an extremely simple but dramatic manner. David trusted God, and because David's faith in God the Father to provide was unquestioned, God showed the whole world what he can do with a willing and able servant, a leather sling and five smooth stones. God loves soldiers and warriors and looks out for us when we trust in his counsel and ability.

Here's a final illustration from Matthew 8:5–13 where a Roman centurion approaches Jesus concerning an ill servant:

> And when Jesus was entered into Capernaum, there came unto him a centurion, beseeching him,
> And saying, Lord, my servant lieth at home sick of the palsy, grievously tormented.
> And Jesus saith unto him, I will come and heal him.
> The centurion answered and said, Lord, I am not worthy that thou shouldest come under my roof: but speak the word only, and my servant shall be healed.
> For I am a man under authority, having soldiers under me: and I say to this man, Go, and he goeth; and to another, Come, and he cometh; and to my servant, Do this, and he doeth it.
> When Jesus heard it, he marvelled, and said to them that followed, Verily I say unto you, I have not found so great faith, no, not in Israel.
> And I say unto you, That many shall come from the east and west, and shall sit down with Abraham, and Isaac, and Jacob, in the kingdom of heaven.

But the children of the kingdom shall be cast out into outer darkness: there shall be weeping and gnashing of teeth.

And Jesus said unto the centurion, Go thy way; and as thou hast believed, so be it done unto thee. And his servant was healed in the selfsame hour. (KJV, 2011)

This centurion was a heathen, a Roman soldier. Though he was a soldier, yet he was a godly man. No man's calling or place will be an excuse for unbelief and sin. See how he states his servant's case. We should concern ourselves for the souls of our children and servants who are spiritually sick, who feel not spiritual evils, who know not that which is spiritually good, and we should bring them to Christ by faith and prayers. Observe his self-abasement. Humble souls are made humbler by Christ's gracious dealings with them. Observe his great faith. The more reserved we are of ourselves, the stronger our confidence in Christ.

Herein, the centurion owns him to have divine power, and a full command of all the creatures and powers of nature, as a master over his servants. Such servants we all should be to God; we must go and come according to the directions of his word and the disposals of his providence. But when the Son of man comes, he finds little faith, therefore he finds little fruit. An outward profession may cause us to be called children of the kingdom, but if we rest in that and have nothing else to show, we shall be cast out. The servant got a cure for his disease, and the master got the approval of his faith. What was said to him is said to all: believe and you shall receive, only believe.

See the power of Christ and the power of faith. The healing of our souls is at once the effect and evidence of our interest in the blood of Christ.

Chapter 13

# VALLEYS

Let us think back to basic training and the instruction we received for map reading and terrain. For most of us, we learned how to read the post or base map, what the symbols and colors represent. But for this chapter, I ask you to look at your fist. Remember? The knuckles from left to right represent a ridge, each knuckle a hilltop, and the low spots between hills a saddle. Now turn your fist sideways and open it forming a *C*. Do you see the line running along the joints from one end to the other, the low spot between your finger pads? There's the valley. If you remember, we learned never to stay there long, but as military history shows, our enemies chose these spots to lure us in and attack from the high ground.

Valley Forge, the Battle of Shenandoah, San Juan Heights, the Marne, and Aisne Valleys, the Ruhr Valley, Chosin Reservoir, A Shau Valley, Euphrates River Valley, and Korengal Valley. Since the earliest days of our country's inception, the United States military fought within a valley of every major war, from the Revolutionary War to the Global War on Terrorism. American Forces fought *uphill* in nearly every battle to take their respective objectives or held the lowest part of the valley against a numerically superior foe. Many of us know these places, walked these places, and remember these places. I did not list them to elicit emotion; I chose them as a reminder that *we* do our best work when the odds seem stacked against us, and we still find a way to win!

So how does knowing about valleys help find peace in our lives? If we think about it for just a moment, we know the answer. Many of us remember a familiar passage of scripture: "Yea, though I walk through the valley of the shadow of death, I will fear no evil: for thou art with me; thy rod and thy staff they comfort me" (Psalm 23:4 KJV, 2011). Very few of us can honestly say that this verse was not somewhere close by, most likely bookmarked in our Bibles by the person or people who gave one to us prior to embarking on a flight overseas.

But let us consider this: the entire chapter of Psalm 23 points to achieving peace by simply trusting God. Let me explain my reasoning: it starts off easy enough—"The Lord is my shepherd." Those who believe receive teaching on how to express satisfaction with the care shown by the universe's greatest Pastor, the one we call Holy Redeemer, and man's Preserver. We rejoice in the knowledge we possess a shepherd with the name of Jehovah. We, a flock of gentle and harmless sheep, graze in emerald pastures receiving care from an alert, professional, and tender shepherd serves as an example to believers how the Shepherd cares and protects our souls.

The greatest abundance is but a dry pasture to a wicked man who relishes in it only what pleases the senses, but to a godly man, who by faith tastes the goodness of God in all his enjoyments, though he has but little of the world, it is a green pasture. The Lord gives quiet and contentment in the mind whatever the situation. We remain blessed with the green pastures of God's Law, let us not think it enough to pass through them, but let us abide in them. The consolations of the Holy Spirit are the still waters by which the saints are led—the streams which flow from the Fountain of living waters. Those only are led by the still waters of comfort who walk in the paths of righteousness. The way of duty is a truly pleasant way—the work of righteousness in peace. In these paths, we cannot walk, unless God leads us into them and leads us on in them. Discontent and distrust proceed from unbelief; an unsteady walk is a consequence. Let us then simply trust our Shepherd's care and hearken to his voice.

The valley of the shadow of death may denote the most severe and terrible affliction or dark dispensation of providence that the psalmist ever could come under. Between the part of the flock on earth and that which is gone to heaven, death lies like a dark valley that must be passed in going from one to the other. But even in this, there are words which lessen the terror. It is but the shadow of death; the shadow of a serpent will not sting nor the shadow of a sword kill. It is a valley deep, indeed, and dark and miry, but valleys are often fruitful, and so is death itself fruitful of comforts to God's people. It is a walk through it; they shall not be lost in this valley but get safe to the mountain on the other side. Death is a king of terrors, but not to the sheep of Christ.

When they come to die, God will rebuke the enemy; he will guide them with his rod and sustain them with his staff. There is enough in the gospel to comfort the saints when dying, and underneath them are the everlasting arms. The Lord's people feast at his table upon the provisions of his love. Satan and wicked men are not able to destroy their comforts while they are anointed with the Holy Spirit and drink of the cup of salvation which is ever full.

Experience teaches believers to trust that the goodness and mercy of God will follow them all the days of their lives; it is their desire and determination to seek their happiness in the service of God here, and they hope to enjoy his love forever in heaven. While here, the Lord can make any situation pleasant by the anointing of his Spirit and the joys of his salvation. But those that would be satisfied with the blessings of his house must keep close to the duties of it.

Chapter 14

# MOUNTAINS

To echo the spirit of the previous chapter, like valleys, mountains played an important part in the military history of the armed forces. Ethan Allen's Green Mountain Boys of Vermont during the Revolutionary War, Lookout, and Kennesaw Mountain during the Civil War, and San Juan and Kettle Hills during the Spanish-American War. United States troops saw no action in the mountains of World War I but served with distinction in the Apennines during World War II, Battle Mountain and Chosin Reservoir during Korea, and admirably in the Central Highlands of Vietnam.

Additionally, the armed forces served with allied war-riors in the Zagros Mountains in Iraq and Adi Ghar and Tora Bora mountain ranges in Afghanistan. Mountains represent a most valued piece of strategic real estate—a vantage point to watch one's enemies as well as provide overwatch for friendly and supportive towns and villages; it is a natural obstacle that revises attack plans or diverts movement.

The Bible refers to mountains, an elevated mass of land most often used as shrines and "high places" 167 times, and Mounts Hermon, Carmel, Olives, Gerizim, Ebal, Gilboa, Sinai, and Seir list as some of the memorable ones. The mentioning of mountains starts with Genesis 7:20 and flows through the entire Bible culminating in Revelations 17:9—a tangible, powerful, and majestic testimony to God's power and mastery of the earth. Many of the first Bible stories we heard as children involving mountains referred to Abraham and Isaac, Moses and the Ten Commandments, Joshua acquiring Mount Hebron as his family home, and Jesus preaching and feeding the five thousand on the Mount.

Consider this: in each example, I mentioned a gift sent by God to the world of man. Because of his faith in God, Abraham received his own son; Moses received God's Law and the standard of living for humanity. Joshua received his portion of the promised land, and five thousand people received food after a miracle involving five fish and two loaves of bread.

Mountains serve as beacons, as a point of reference when seeking a destination. Hard to miss a prominent landmark that not only dominates the landscape but reaches into the sky. Is it any wonder that God uses them to emphasize his thoughts and actions when dealing with us? Additionally, mountains appear remote, formidable, and serve as a quiet place for a man to commune with God. Abraham, Moses, Joshua, David, and Jesus knew this, choosing mountains as prayer closets and each speaking to God as an act of obedience.

The psalmist wrote, "Before the mountains were brought forth, or ever thou hadst formed the earth and the world, even from everlasting to everlasting, thou art God" (Psalm 90:2 KJV). David acknowledges God's eternal existence before the foundation of the earth, the mountains not even a divine thought. Can we not do the same? Have we not seen the beauty God creates when we stand on a mountain and observe a sunrise or sunset? I know I have, and I give him thanks and praise for allowing me to see and experience it.

Chapter 15

# BATTLE BUDDY

The United States Army implemented a "Battle Buddy" program many years ago, revamping and improving its effectiveness by reinforcing the concept of "team" at the smallest unit level. The expectations of a battle buddy involve assisting his or her partner both in and out of combat as well as providing comradeship and motivation. A true battle buddy watches the back of his or her partner, offers words of praise when a partner excels, and provides criticism when that partner fouls up. Battle buddies laugh, cry, fight, and take care of one another in a manner that the average person will never understand.

This relationship, however, often changes because one partner receives a promotion, transfers to a new unit, or receives a new duty station assignment; the word *finite* is an apt description to the end of their union. But there remains one Battle Buddy who lives within you, offers encouragement and counsel, provides guidance and calm during times of turmoil, and he goes by the name of the Holy Spirit. Even before your birth, the Holy Spirit took up residence within you, watched over you, and sowed the seeds of friendship. He stayed with you through school, spoke to your soul as you matured, and set the table for the eventual meeting with the one known as "The Great I Am." I will not forget my battle buddies and their collective friendship, but the Holy Spirit and I possess a relationship that transcends even the best of these.

The power of the Holy Spirit and his abilities exceed human comprehension; our understanding of him comes solely from Scripture. The Bible tells us that the Holy Spirit possesses a distinctive personality, a member of the Trinity, said by Jesus himself in Matthew 28:19–20 (KJV), "Go ye therefore, and teach all nations, baptizing them in the name of the Father, and of the Son, and of the Holy Ghost: Teaching them to observe all things whatsoever I have commanded you: and, lo, I am with you always, even unto the end of the world. Amen."

Man benefits greatly from the work of the Holy Spirit. Psalm 104:30 tells us, "Thou sendest forth thy spirit, they are created: and thou renewest the face of the earth." In other words, when it comes to the creation of life, the Holy Spirit serves as the immediate source. Who better to call a battle buddy than the one there at your conception?

The original best friend simply tasked with bringing you and me into existence. The Holy Spirit helped conceive Jesus Christ within Mary as evidenced in Luke 1:35: "And the angel answered and said unto her, The Holy Ghost shall come upon thee, and the power of the Highest shall overshadow thee: therefore also that holy thing which shall be born of thee shall be called the Son of God." I think this act alone solidifies the Holy Spirit's position as the ultimate battle buddy. But there's so much more to the Holy Spirit than just the act of conception; He reveals scriptural truth and serves as the divine source of inspiration to the writers of the Bible. The Apostle Paul reinforces this truth in 2 Timothy 3:16–17:

All scripture is given by inspiration of God and is profitable for doctrine, for reproof, for correction, for instruction in righteousness: That the man of God may be perfect, thoroughly furnished unto all good works. (KJV, 2016)

And because he remains the single source for inspiration of God's Word as well as its author (Ephesians 6:17), the Holy Spirit takes an active role in ensuring we, as his battle buddies, embrace salvation (Romans 1:16), receive conversion and sanctification (Acts 20:32), and *believe* that he lives within us (Romans 8:9).

The Holy Spirit gives us power and motivates us when we feel weak, emboldens us to speak without fear, and guides us in times of uncertainty, and reminds us that he has our back, just like our service battle buddy.

I understand you hold some skepticism about the existence of the Holy Spirit, but I assure you he is very real, and he works on your heart, mind, and soul. He makes life worth living and encourages us to seek out the love of Christ. He never leaves you, and when times get tough, he remains steadfast, never flinching or wavering. He exemplifies the best and honorable character traits and personifies the concept of courage. When you need a battle buddy, no one fills that role better than the Holy Spirit; you can count on that and him.

Chapter 16

# TRUST AND OBEY

When each of us enlisted or commissioned, we took an oath, officers slightly different from the following excerpt but still just as powerful and meaningful.

> I, _____, do solemnly swear (or affirm) that I will support and defend the Constitution of the United States against all enemies, foreign and domestic; that I will bear true faith and allegiance to the same; and that I will obey the orders of the President of the United States and the orders of the officers appointed over me, according to regulations and the Uniform Code of Military Justice. So, help me God. (Title 10, US Code; Act of 5 May 1960 replacing the wording first adopted in 1789, with amendment effective 5 October 1962, [Powers, 2019]).

We took this oath to solidify our commitment to whatever branch of the military we chose, and we gave our word to "obey the orders of the president of the United States and the orders of the officers appointed over me…" The oath says nothing about *liking* either the president or the officers in the chain of command, but it does *expect* obedience to the commands of both. I am not suggesting blind obedience; we must use common sense and clear judgment when receiving a questionable or unlawful order and then act accordingly.

However, when receiving a clear and lawful order, we comply and obey. Obedience does not require much effort, and when God asks us to do something, we need to do it. Obedience to God not only pleases him but also it serves as a means of communication as well as establishes a pattern of acceptable behavior. This good behavior, in turn, fosters a relationship of love and trust.

The Bible exhorts us to trust and obey; in 2 Samuel 22:2–4, King David writes,

> And he [David] said, The Lord [is] my rock, and my fortress, and my deliverer; The God of my rock; in him will I trust: [he is] my shield, and the horn of my salvation, my high tower, and my refuge, my saviour; thou savest me from violence. I will call on the Lord, [who is] worthy to be praised: so shall I be saved from mine enemies. (KJV, 2016)

David wrote this as a psalm of praise; those trusting God in the way of duty find him a reliable assistant in times

of great and perilous danger. We especially mention mirac-
ulous or divine preservations in our praises, but we also
need to remember that until we enter heaven, complete
deliverance from our enemies does not occur on earth. God
makes good on this promise supported by Paul's writing of
2 Timothy 4:18: "And the Lord shall deliver me from every
evil work, and will preserve me unto his heavenly kingdom:
to whom be glory for ever and ever. Amen" (KJV, 2016).

The Bible uses the words *trust* 188 times and *obey*
115—a total of 303 instances that fully support the belief
that surrendering one's life to God perfectly illustrates trust
and obedience. Easier said than done; many of us cannot
relinquish total control of our lives to God because we
either do not fully comprehend the benefits of doing so or
we possess such a tight grip on our life that letting go scares
us or makes us panic.

Chapter 17

# AAR

Now the mission seems complete, and we need time to sit down, reflect on what we did, and how to either improve or continue what we did. The military calls this an AAR or after-action review. You read the book, understood the concepts, and possibly applied some of it to your own life. I graciously thank you for doing all those things, but I think a review can never hurt, especially if doing so saves even one of the twenty-two who tragically take their own lives.

When we participated in after-action reviews, the facilitator reminded us of a few things:

1. Be honest.
2. Rank means nothing here.
3. No thick skins.

The leader of the session, if you remember, was usually an OC/observer controller, and he or she recited the mission, the objectives, and whether we achieve or fail to meet expectations and standards. Then the real fun starts with the addition of a dry erase easel, marker(s), and the headliners of "Sustain" and "Improve."

For the uninitiated, the two categories of sustain and improve represent things during the operation that we wish to continue or sustain and those things we must do better to achieve our objectives or improve. In my experience, providing instances or tasks to sustain requires little effort. It's always good to know what you do well, but things to improve generally require a bit more thought. No one wants to openly admit they do something incorrectly or fail to achieve an objective because of a shortcoming, but to grow and learn, one needs to acknowledge these things nonetheless.

The facilitator usually chooses the lowest ranking man to provide at least one comment for each section, and those comments generally reflect what we already know; sometimes, that private offers up something unexpected and yet relevant. I challenge you to take a quiet moment; reflect on your situation, and come up with an unexpected but relevant answer. I just ask you to follow the AAR rules.

Only you know the relevance and importance of the information in this book on your life, and I hope that some portion helps in some way. I feel like sharing my faith, thoughts, opinions, and relatable information to all of you serve as credence to the sincerity of my motives. I believe everyone needs God, to walk with Jesus, remain humble, show kindness, and talk with him daily. To achieve these goals, one must employ and perform these regularly; a habit in and of itself takes at least twenty-one days to stick. Give it a try, and I promise you the personal rewards you receive and the changes to your life make you happy and lead toward a sense of peace.

*So are you ready to take up your ruck and follow Jesus?*

# AFTERWORD

This project represents a labor of love and represents the fight within me to complete it—four years of contemplation, self-evaluation, and yes, procrastination. I learned a great deal about myself and asked God to help me find a way to finish this.

It does not matter how many people read it; even if just one person receives a blessing from it, then I achieved my goal. Helping people is important; the year 2020 showed us that with the outbreak of COVID-19. I could no longer allow this project to remain dormant on a thumb drive, and I prayed for help, guidance, and strength to get it done. God blessed me along the way, and I am eternally grateful.

My personal goal is that you found something, anything from these words to apply to your life, and my sincerest hope is that you found God, asked him into your heart, and received the blessed assurance of salvation.

It has been my distinct honor and pleasure to write this book, to share personal details and anecdotes, and provide a basic path toward healing and a happier, healthier life.

# REFERENCES

No Author. 2018. "Praise" retrieved from http://www.dictionary.com/browse/praise?s=t.

No Author. 2018. Isaiah 26:3 Retrieved from https://www.biblestudytools.com/philippians/4–7.html.

No Author. 2019. Job 36:10–12. Retrieved from https://www.kingjamesbibleonline.org/Job-Chapter-36/#12.

Powers, Rod. 2019. "Oath of Enlistment for Military Service" Retrieved from https://www.thebalancecareers.com/oath-of-enlistment-3354049.

Sherman, William Tecumseh. 1880. "War Is Hell!" Retrieved from http://www.military-quotes.com/william-sherman.htm.

United States Army. 2017. "FRAGO" Retrieved from http://www.armystudyguide.com/content/Leadersbook_information/Combat_Leaders_Guide/plan-fragmentary-order-fr-2.shtml.

United States Army. 2017. "OPORD" Retrieved from http://www.armystudyguide.com/content/Leadersbook_information/Combat_Leaders_Guide/plan-operations-order-fr-2.shtml.

# ABOUT THE AUTHOR

Dana Paul McCloud lives in Clarkesville, Georgia, with his wife Brandy and dog Ace. They've been married nine years and enjoy hiking and spending time at the lake fishing. Dana served in the military for over twenty-five years, splitting service with the Georgia and Vermont Army National Guard. He retired in October 2014 at the rank of sergeant.